BLUE NUMBERS, RED LIFE

Roy Jacobstein

Blue Numbers, Red Life is the winner of the 2000 Harperprints
Chapbook Competition sponsored by the North Carolina Writers'
Network.

Final Judge: Gregory Orr
Preliminary Judges: Anthony S. Abbott and Robin Greene

Publication of this chapbook was made possible with the
sponsorship and production assistance of Harperprints,
the award-winning commercial printer in Henderson, N.C.,
and by a grant from the North Carolina Arts Council.

Cover painting: "Chasm" by Mindy Weisel. Used by kind
permission of the artist.

Cover design: Margaret Rabb

Copyright © 2000 by Roy Jacobstein

Published and distributed by
The North Carolina Writers' Network
PO Box 954, Carrboro, NC 27510   ISBN# 1-883314-12-7

—For Linda and David

ACKNOWLEDGEMENTS

Grateful acknowledgement is made to the editors of the following publications where these poems, some of which have been revised, first appeared:

The Beloit Poetry Journal: "What It Was"

Graven Images: "The Lesson"

Green Mountains Review: "The Cardplayers"

Gulf Coast: "Home Run"

JAMA: "Dutch Landscape"

Luna: "La Création"

The Marlboro Review: "Reincarnation" (runner-up, 1999 Marlboro Prize in Poetry)

Mediphors: "Admissions"

Mid-American Review: "Swale" (winner, 1999 James Wright Poetry Prize)

Nimrod: "Passover," "There Is No Point in Time"

Poet Lore: "#8 Approaches"

Prairie Schooner: "Sto Lat"

Puerto del Sol: "Calamari"

Quarterly West: "Rooting"

Sarasota Review of Poetry: "Morning Flight"

Sundog: "Across from Holy Name Hospital"

The Threepenny Review: "Bypass"

Witness: "Atomic Numbers," "Near Rusomo,"
   "'Squid's Sex Life Revealed' in *USA TODAY*"

Wordwrights: "Magnetic Field," "Time-Lapse"

Over and over something would remain.

—James Merrill, "For Proust"

CONTENTS

One

Two

One

Bypass

One day it's Miss Scarlet with
the Candlestick in the Conservatory,
the next they're carting someone
down the corridor to where Dr. Black
with the chisel in the O.R.
waits to crack the vault of a chest.
It's not a calico cat, purring
all night by a child's side,
not acne, not the daily rush
to the job, it's a gurney pulsing
along a narrow passageway,
and it seems you are that someone
for whom the Heart Team scrubs,
a corpuscle the color of dusk,
wanting for air, and no clue
how you got there, nor who waits
so silently behind the next door,
Colonel Mustard or Professor Plum,
come to the Ballroom with the Rope.

Atomic Numbers

Mr. Gardner in 10th grade told us there was no purpose
to mitochondria, just function. Your lungs turn black
in a day if you smoke, black as that ink streaking your
sorry hands, thundered bald Mr. Strepek in Print Shop,
and stay black five years, even if a cigarette never touches
your lips again, and your breath stinks too. But Karen took
Home Ec., so she kept flicking Virginia Slims from the pack,
blowing onion rings into my face. Miss Testasecca taught
the degrees of the right angle equal those of the other two
angles in a right triangle. Miss Piilo made us memorize
atomic numbers. Uranium: Number 235—no wonder
it's radioactive. Pb, sign for lead, stood for something
like *plumbus* in Latin—or was it Greek? After semester break
she came back Mrs. Giglio. *Lily,* she said it meant in Italian,
turning to write a formula on the blackboard, tugging
at her tightened skirt. Things're getting tougher all the time,
Chucky Klein quipped. Years later he got himself shot
reporting Jonestown, survived, moved to TV. I want to pop
a hand up to old Mr. Curran right now—How come *The Lord
of the Flies* has to have Piggy drop those glasses and why
did that 17 year-old leave her newborn girl in the dumpster
last week and what'll they do to her now? Who's the *rough
beast,* he'd ask in that brogue that caressed us like the tongue
of a cat. Some days you just want to be toes, curled inward
or pressed against another warm body until first recess crawls
by—then Mr. Adamson's supposed to teach us how to shift
from second to third and accelerate into the straightaway.

Admissions

To do ... to doo ... what to doo,
to doo ... I don't know what
to doo, to doo ... to dooo, moans

Hector nonstop, his moans curling
counterclockwise along the corridor,
dragging us with him through his day-

long night, as we interns round on
the latest admissions: the cheerleader
O.D.'d on spurned love and Tylenol,

the seizure disorder from Hornell—
not epilepsy, a visitation from God,
his mother says, *the one who knows*

me and wants to paint me as Jesus
(long hair, black beard, and all).
In the treatment room they're piercing

the spine of the next new leukemic:
her back curves across the exam table
like a piece of ripe cantaloupe

awaiting a serrated knife. Above us,
TVs flicker—another game show.
Nurses wheel drug carts, I.V. poles;

shift succeeds shift. Over everything,
that ceaseless droning—Hector Arroyo,
age 9, demented, gone to encephalitis.

And at the rear of the little troupe,
fingering his stethoscope's dark rubber
the way a snake-charmer fingers his flute,

a 25 year-old boy sweating his lines, sweat
lining the back of his short white coat, a secret
charter member of *The Hector Arroyo Club*

who wonders what they'll stick into *him*
when no cobra dances from the straw basket.

What It Was

Often, at Strong Memorial Hospital,
I'd guide a 15-gauge needle into the center
of a child's lower back. It was so easy,
any time I wanted I could slip it in,
between the vertebral ridges of L2 and L3,
blindfolded even, feel the pop, and presto!:
cerebrospinal fluid dripping out. I never once
fooled the nurses into believing the kid—say, Mona
or Phil—didn't have acute leukemia. They knew
the drill: slap on the purple label,
call the *stat* messenger, console the parents
waiting for the test results, a flotilla
of 100,000 deranged cells per cubic centimeter
pouring from Mona's marrow or Phil's spleen
into the bloodstream. After my latest 36-hour day,
sun risen, set, risen, set, I'd arrive home,
smelling of night rattles and slow clocks
and sodden scrambled eggs, and slip
into my then-wife's arms, wanting only
to be told what it wasn't. But all she said
before I went under, again swimming her reefs
without aqualung or mask, was what it was.

Dutch Landscape

—for Roelf Padt

You lie upstairs in a king-sized bed
as fluid the color of weak tea
seeps into your pleural cavities
and stains your breath.
In the living room below,
your son, Simon—*sea-moan* in Dutch—
pedals his red trike in circles
on the bare wood floor
and Piaf hunkers at my feet—

Piaf, who frisked down center aisle
of the Pieterskerk and leapt
when we threw the rice.
Beyond the long window
a lone duck drifts
across the murky water of the Prinsengracht
and the cobblestones glisten,
the way they do here in Amsterdam,
after the rain.

Years ago, working the afternoon
shift at Dodge Main, I fit
the gray lips of the spot welder
over twin plates of steel
twenty-two times an hour.
When I tripped the trigger
arcs of flame fused the plates
in a shower of sparks.

I want to etch this moment
of you fast into hard metal,
to solder your body
to something with roots,
in spite of knowing
I can weld life to no one,
no one to life.

Across from Holy Name Hospital

What's semiotics to a cat?
Splayed on your lap, her four limbs
to the four winds, no language

conditions her thought, no doubt
the bobbing branch bobs. She takes it
all in, all of it her due, until *better*

tempts those tawny semaphores
ever attuned to what is, and she's off,
leaving us to our signs, words:

Quiet, Zone, needle, mass.
True, there's still the world rolling
from your nib, the world you make

as you like, a world of whatever
you choose to fix: cinnamon toast,
or purple crocus, bent on return.

You can make anything you want,
you can call anything out, have it
scutter past in the mist—

sand crab, storm cloud, cat, Mother
Superior (wimple and jowl)—
anything at all, but the gone

remain gone, all the holy names.

—Ethel Ippolito, 1933-1998

Magnetic Field

Sixteen years, Doug, you dumb fuck.
Sixteen years ago—not on a day
like today: gray, planed by wind,
squeezed in the vise of February,
violet worms clotting the sidewalk,
the dank air, with their earth-slime
stink, a day anyone could fathom
sighting down the wrong end
of twin barrels.
                No, one of those
days of blossom, an irruption
of rhododendron and redbud,
one of those days lovers crave.
You should know the eyelids
Dad passed on to both of us
sag, Doug, just like his did,
and the crows that still blacken
our sycamores caw *ought, ought.*

Near Rusomo

— *A.P. Wire Photo, New York Times, 12/21/97*

— *People say they have to express their emotions.*
I'm sick of that. Photography doesn't teach you
to express your emotions; it teaches you how to see.
Berenice Abbott

They're downstream now,
beyond the falls,
eight or ten, or more,
out of the turbulence.
The Kagera River churns
onward into Tanzania, leaving
them behind in the backwash.
The smooth stone outcropping
of their native land hovers
over them like a mother seal.
They huddle against her
black flanks the way they leaned
into one another last week
in the Church for safety
in numbers. And now
that the machetes have passed,
the torsos are looking down
into the debris-choked shallows
for their missing heads and limbs.

Sto Lat

> —"*Long life,*" *the Polish toast to good health,*
> *literally, "one hundred years."*

> — *To the memory of Robert Desnos*

Your "Voice" comes late, Robert, here
in a converted barn at a writers' conference,
amid the litany of concentration camps
rattling the loose windows, the names
of many unknown to me, a child
of the mild and mundane Midwest, born
after the ovens had cooled, their vapors
curling no longer out of Europe's voiceless mouth,
over the Black Madonna's saltless tears.

There were blue numbers on the ventral surface
of her right arm, my mother-in-law-to-be,
that spring day in 1970. Her daughter, Shoshana,
the one the few survivors from Radom
said was *Mania's exact double,*
stood beneath the canopy, Detroit Shaarey Zedek,
and heard the rabbi say "Repeat after me in Hebrew
and then English: *Anee l'dodee v'dodee lee—*
I am my beloved's as my beloved is mine."
It was a time of learning new words
like *lesion, necrosis, dysmorphic, ventral.*

I pay tribute to you Mania, Manushka, Maria,
grandmother of my son,
I thank God you spoke flawlessly
that guttural tongue I can never hear
without hearing *round them up,*
spoke so fluently you and your blue eyes passed,
and even when they could pass no longer,
still, at Auschwitz, they were password
to the office job, the occasional German kindness
of warm roll, a hard-boiled egg,

just as there must have been at Auschwitz
a sunny day, sunny days,
the kind of day where anywhere on Earth
long life seems possible.

I pay tribute to you, Robert,
reading the fortunes of your fellow travelers—headed
where?—Birkenau, Belsen, Treblinka, Terezin?
Even in the boxcars you trailed your index finger
along the smooth palms of the young,
the creases and fissures of the old,
predicting in a low voice, over the clacketing rails,
in French, your mother tongue, the language
of Piaf and Pétain, to one and all, *long life.*

To all those smiling Cambodians
to whom I spoke in stilting Khmer
in the refugee camps at Khao-I-Dang and Nong Khai,
and those in the transit camp at Pinatnikom, the ones
whose smile Pol Pot could not efface,
behind whose teeth every tongue,
every bitten tongue, held its tale of loss
(buried in the graceful splay of the dancers' fingers,
the artificial fingernails, curved backward, painted gold,
the dances for birth, for rebirth, for harvest): tribute.

To that one specific woman, her name long flown,
who came to the makeshift delivery room, abdomen swollen
well beyond the nine-month gravid girth
the obstetrics text told us to expect,
and delivered, without anesthesia, without a sound,
a boy without a brain, and got up off the table
and smiled at me, made the *wai* of respect,
eyes cast down, palms pressed above her bowed head,
and, still saying nothing, returned
to the straw pallet in the thatched-roof tent
where her husband and mother and child awaited her,
where she'd slept each night the past two years: tribute.

It is true—the hacked and mutilated in Kigali,
the *ethnically cleansed* in all the Srebenicas,
those who survived the Gulag and those who didn't,
the *desaparacidos* of Santiago and Buenos Aires
and the bloody broken wishbone of Central America,
those who fell at Wounded Knee and those who yet stand,
the children of the children of the children
of the slaves who passed through Gorée Island
to become New World dust,
the Armenians Palestinians Tibetans Kashmiris Kurds—
all the tongues, all the words: poetry stops nothing.

I don't know when you were born, Robert.
You wrote the poem we heard today in 1926,
the one where you call out at midnight,
call all to you: *those lost in the fields ...*
old skeletons ... young oaks cut down ...
scraps of cloth rotting on the ground ...
tornadoes and hurricanes ...
the smoke of volcanoes ...
hangmen pilots bricklayers architects
assassins
the one you love,
you call the one you love,
three times you call the one you love.

Yours is the poem of a young man,
but not a youth. I'd guess you are thirty, maybe
twenty-nine, born in 1897, one hundred years ago.
If they found you in some café, arguing
about Wittgenstein or Nietzsche with your friends,
if you didn't look like a Jew
and none of your neighbors bore you a grudge
or coveted your flat or your goose-neck lamp,
maybe they didn't find you for a while,
until 1942 or 1943. That would make you
my age when you boarded the train.

In the grainy flickering silent movie of your life
it would be winter, a gray day, raked by wind,
your black fedora slung low over your brow,
but it wasn't, I can see it, one of those perfect
Parisian days, late spring, 11 a.m.,
the smell of *brioche* caressing the cobblestones,
the sun bending to kiss the dry earth
like a pilgrim first arrived to Mecca.

Soon we enter the next century.
All the future names God alone knows—their names,
the towns, the rivers which will run black—God
and you, Robert, and the darkmost chamber
of every human heart, but you knew all that
even as you went up that rough planking
into the boxcar, and stood with the others
massed there, held on to the side boards
with one hand, the other you took
from your lower back, where the blunt end
of the *Polizei*'s rifle had smashed
into your kidney, your urine will run red,
all this you knew
when you ran your finger along the wrinkled right palm
of the woman with the gold tooth,
looked deep into her deep brown eyes
and predicted *long life*,
and to her twelve-year-old grandson clinging to her side,
long life.

I want to tell you
that twelve-year-old was my father,
someone's father,
you are right, we do
have long life.

The wheel is turning, Robert.
The next century is upon us.
The knives are glinting and sharp.
The one you loved did not listen.
The one you loved did not hear.
The one you loved did not answer.
I extend my hand to you.

Two

Reincarnation

If they're right, this mosquito dive-bombing my ear
into total *presence* at 3 a.m. is Rasputin, or your late

Schnauzer, or possibly (why not?) one of those spears
of asparagus served at Cousin Dee's 83rd birthday

luncheon last month, or even Cousin Dee herself,
depending on karmic law and the minute particulars

of transmigration of the soul (interval of dormancy,
if any, distance traversed in space and time, degree

of ascent or descent on the biologic scale from mite
to man, etc.), which means among this newly-hatched

crop of anophelines, only the females of which bite,
and which unimpeded live but a few days, could be

Shakespeare (spiraled down through the centuries) or
the louse that once bit the arse of the unknown (to us)

object of his affections in *Sonnet 55*, so on the chance
those who believe this sort of thing—a priori no less

nor more plausible than Red Seas parting or virgin
births or sun gods demanding sacrifice of human

(preferably young and female) flesh—are right,
I'll forbear from further attempts to squash what

well may be Mohandas K. Gandhi, secure in knowing
should I come back as a cat I'll sleep soundly, curled

upon myself on the soft couch while someone's
cousin or mother or child circles overhead

in her newfound brown body, shaking the last
of her human tears from her glistening wings ...

The Cardplayers

Of course the dead hover close—take my
first cousin, Nelson: he's to be buried later

this morning in a city 500 miles from here.
The rabbi will chant the age-old prayers,

those who remain will provide solace.
I know: my mother and father and brother—

cardplayers too—shuffled from the Earth
to the same ceremony. They're here now

in the kitchen. It's my father's deal.
Already Nelson is pulling up his chair,

cutting the deck. Listen to the metal legs
scraping the linoleum, the flutter of the cards

as they fall onto the beige folding table,
the clink of the ice in their glasses,

their laughter filling the living room,
the still air, the red irretrievable dawn.

Rooting

Ardent *Cingané*, gypsy in Turkish,
my three-legged calico cat, presses
her pink nose into my warm armpit.

This must be the single-minded way
pigs in Perigord bulldoze autumn
earth awake in search of truffles,

black as tar, more valuable than gold.
It must be the way the eyes
of that five-year old boy who once

was me raked the munificent grass
for the buried treasure of bottle caps,
his useless clod of an infant brother

nursing away atop an Army blanket.
In Rome, the cells where gladiators
awaited release into the sun-stippled

Colisseum remain darkened, silted-in.
In the *Living* section of yesterday's *Times*,
archaeologists in Jerusalem sift bits

of pre-Canaanite pottery. And somewhere,
in some damp persistent cellar, a poet
roots the humus of memory for the precise

image that will trigger the flow of milk.

Passover

Humming to herself, my oldest aunt,
Bea, ladles *knadlach*: matzoh-ball boulders
plopping into a yellow globular sea.

Soon all four aunts will rise in unison,
on some arcane cue, to clump again
in the kitchen—that long unbroken lineage:

shtetl and sister and steam. Pinochle
will claim the uncles, cousins will scatter,
some to swap baseball cards, others

to dress dolls, but I'll return to the photos,
fixed between those little black triangles.
Here's Uncle Herman's bayonet, gleaming

in the Prussian sun. This one is Uncle Saul,
in the shadows of steerage, his four-tongued
goodbye to Smyrna already swallowed down.

And over here, on that railroad platform,
the slim teenager singing for the last Tsar—
Nicholas II, sitting so straight between

his uniformed guards on the royal train—
that's Aunt Bea, at the front of the chorus
of village girls spilling out their dark eyes.

Time-Lapse

Bomber jacket, billowy white scarf,
leather headgear lining his unlined
forehead, light haloing his pupils—
he's ready to face the Lüftwaffe solo.
When visitors ask his story, I tell
of missions over Germany: the Flying

Fortresses opening their bays onto Essen
as he and his P-51 Mustang duel
the Messerschmidts over the Ruhr,
four of those babies flaming down, down—
four more to be rounded up for scrap;
his three kills in the raids on Regensburg;
Berlin, again and again, flares
in the night sky, the ack-ack, the tracers.

How many takes did they take at
            The Bach Studio
                SIKESTON
                  MO
              June 1943
father? How many days left until

final flight training, your slow slide
from the dusty runway, straight
to the base library to check books
out to officers the duration of the War?
In a darkroom, what dodgings
are needed to airbrush fear?

#8 Approaches

Oh, to circle back whence we come,
figure of eight, round palindrome,
perfection of mirror and return.
Were we waiting in Mantua or Milan
for this school bus, we'd be waiting
for *otto*, umbrellaed against the *pioggia*.
Today would be *oggi*, your first day
at the *scuola* in the language of Dante.

But autumn would still be streaking
your yellow slicker, your soft palm
would yet fit in mine, your laugh
fill my chest no more in Tuscany
than Albany, and I'd be waiting
for you, wherever your feet alit,
whenever the bumblebee door buzzed
open, just as it now buzzes shut.

The Lesson

What transgression, Bobby Bordley,
what transgression made fat Mr. Hantler
drop his trowel, his gloves, everything
he was doing that hot May day
to chase you from one end
of Fullerton to the other, trying to
wring your little neck?

The rest of the *Valiants*
stood stupefied on the sidewalk—
livestock stunned before slaughter,
running only in our minds,
but running with you still,
weaving a desperate curlicue
to evade that grown man.

Nothing from that day remains,
not George V Drugs, not the Avalon Theater,
not Mr. Hantler, younger then, no doubt,
than any *Valiant* now.
Not the roses he trimmed so carefully
and watered with his green snake
of garden hose, nor the ball and curse

you hurled into his flower bed.
And Helen Hantler herself must be gray
and stout and only once or twice
think back to how her legs twitched
behind the screen door
to see someone—anyone—
escape her father's meaty hands.

There Is No Point in Time

A name surfaces like carp in an ornamental pond, rising
from the deep to the grated fish feed of an 8-beat line.
Never be afraid, Proust says, *to go too far, for truth*

lies beyond, hence this call to him, my oldest friend.
Who else would remember Ting, returning the striped
rubber ball, paw over yellow paw? How does it happen,

one moment on a broiling corner, embroiled in another
spat, the next, two decades gone? Does he remember
when we saw *Morocco*, how Dietrich is left to wander

the desert, trailing Gary Cooper's kepi into the gray
celluloid dusk? Does he remember my tiny mother
taught him *Partir, c'est mourir un peu?*[1] I remember

the *lieder* in his living room. His tenor was so pure ...
that voice!—can that *cri du chat*[2] be his? Hang up.
Voices, too, must change. No message to leave, no

big deal, *rien*, what can be said in 20 seconds can be
held inside twenty years, though who can say when
a thought of him will come again, bleeding up to feed.

---

[1]*To part is to die a little.*
[2]*Cat's cry.*

28

Home Run

Somewhere still it's Salami Day,
so my father is slicing and dicing
with the precision of a Japanese chef,

the chunks of purple meat flecked
with white fat piling higher and higher
on the Formica counter in our kitchen.

If it's Tuesday, it's French Fry Day:
my friends are hooking their mitts
to their jeans, hopping onto their bikes.

It's 5 p.m., my father's been sighted,
disgorged from the Dexter-Davison bus.
His briefcase moves in pace with his stride,

up the street toward our first floor flat.
Already they can hear his chortle,
can imagine the gurgle of hot oil

surging through the mesh strainer,
already they're burning the roofs
of their mouths, they'll never learn—

and the golden, hand-hewn fries, edges
beveled like cut gems, taste so good.
They see the tie loosened at his neck,

the sleeves of his white-on-white shirt
rolled back, baring the lipomas
that line the length of his dark forearms

like eroded hills. Sweat pearls on his scalp,
a windshield's first drops of rain: wiped away,
returning. It's the sweat of running the bases,

the ball rolling between left and center
all the way to the fence, it's the good sweat
of a good man: my father, headed home.

Swale

Do you think it would've helped if I'd known *swale*
meant a low-lying or depressed and often wet stretch
of land? Maybe I would have understood her moistures
and stoops, though it's of Scandinavian origin and I'm not.
Ah, origins. I swear we make a mountain of a few inches,
a few cells. If not a mountain, a hillock, a rude mound.
Clit or cock, ermine, stoat, aren't we all just topiary
anyway, on the road to the inner harbor? And speaking
of pruning, why did it take so many years to understand
that sign? Every 5th Thursday, 3:30 p.m., there it was,
across the street from DOM & ERNIE'S, visible as a galaxy
of dust motes in a sun-shaft: *We Repair Non-Union Haircuts.*
Like a rune or sentence in need of a good parsing, I sat
on the cracked red leather of the middle barber's chair,
peering out at it, waiting to be spun around, *voilà*, again
a Mexican Hairless, Dom and my mother doing their polka
of delight, my brain backstroking in the bay of abstraction.
True, its syntax is none too mystic, maybe it was the diction,
how the hell should I know, I was only eight. Befuddlement
was deep in urban Detroit. Don't you love how b and d thud
by? And who could ever forget Henry Ford's goons, the blood
vessels bursting like boils from the auto worker's heads
at the sight of the truncheons, there at the factory overpass?
Well, Dom and Mom could, evidently, probably Ernie too,
hard to say for sure, being he was off Thursdays. Funny,
later I was a Teamster, around the time of the riots. Local 199—
had my union card, but how do we really know we've made
the team? And what's the game, duckpins? And now that we're
approaching the main theme here, what about the problem
of pomegranates—they're so different, and they come from
so far away. Aren't they're just like relationships, extraction
of each insular seed (Lat.: *insula*, island) labor-intensive

to the max. Cock, clit, haircut, union card, Latin, Old Norse,
where does any of it get us, I ask you. It's all so damned runic—
though have you noticed with Whitman Samplers, how
the caramels are in one corner and the nougats in another,
and you can see the curve of the cashews peeking through
the bittersweet, saying in shards of cashew-speak, *pick me.*

Calamari

Listen my son, this is
how it's going to be—one day
you'll be racing from work
at dusk and pass a blue sign
for a restaurant called Mykonos
and you'll remember the *you*
of today, the woman
you're late for, Janice or Jane,
will understand if you pause,
facing the sea of white-
washed wall, the windmill, the shore-
front café where you first tasted
ouzo and squid, *calamari*
they said and you said
the next thirty years,
though you never returned
though the generals fled
and the woman you loved
for her self and her laugh
and her yet-bandaged wrists
left the breeze
that still blows over your body
at odd times like this.

Morning Flight

In a distant city a boy once shared the pig
Wilbur's dismay at all Charlotte's children
streaming from the barnyard that first day

of spring. Like so many jellyfish riding
currents of the Coral Sea, the baby spiders
lifted away from him, into the sunlit breeze.

Today, at a meeting where talk is of profit
and loss, a man thinks of insects he's known—
tiny ants tugging grains of sugar homeward,

mornings in his kitchen, migrating Monarchs
gowning the grove near Santa Cruz in orange
and black silk, a host of spiders in an April

barnyard—and wonders, as he gazes through
frosted panes of aqua glass, if enough webbing
remains within to wind, unwind, cast off again.

"Squid's Sex Life Revealed" in *USA TODAY*

So now they've gone and told everyone
yours is like the rest of ours: "dark and fast,"
a "deep sea mystery ... solved."
They say, *mi amigo*, genus *Architeuthis*,
giant male squid, you "measure 45 feet long
and would make calamari rings bigger
than a tractor tire."
        (Sautéed in olive oil,
spread over a steaming bed of rice,
you'd sate a hungry battalion—lie low,
mon ami, down there in your inky cavern,
half a mile below the sizzling woks.)

They say you "use an extremely muscular penis,
three feet long and functioning like a rivet or nail gun,"
that your "encounters are infrequent and chance."
When passing a female "like two ships
in the night"—
        apologies, my friend, for the unbounded
human appetite for seafood and cliché—
you "quickly maneuver to hammer into one of her arms
and inject under hydraulic pressure,"
your six-inch line of salty sperm
undulating in the pitch.

At last they've captured the bare details,
but what do the scientists know of squid-time,
of how fast your waiting for her passes
in the safe cold shadows,
and how love's tentacles hold.

"La Création"

—Chagall Museum, Nice

Naked, from out the blue vortex,
a grown man lightly borne
in a blue-winged angel's arms
bends his head to the staggering light,
a man newly born, looking
to the world above, the world
of fish and the yellow moon
and the woman curved like a giant red ear,
the red sun, swirling, blown
out of an angel's horn,
the ram-headed man with the red Torah,
the *shtetl*, the rabbi, the ladder,
the menorah's nine lemony flames,
the purple-breasted women,
the blue lyre held by the blue king,
the donkey, lion, goat,
the golden fish with hands for fins,
the bearded butterfly. Above,
above His Son swaying on the white Cross,
flaccid abdomen covered at the groin
by a gray-fringed prayer shawl,
above it all, disembodied, two hands,
the visible hands of hiding
God, proffer twin tablets shaped
like pale loaves, or gravestones,
and I put my arm around my new wife's waist,
and she puts her arm around mine,
and we hold like that a minute
in that white room, in that white light,
infinite wavelets of white light.

NOTES

Bypass. Many Americans of several generations remember rapt hours spent hunched over a game board of CLUE, moving, say, the powder blue token of Mrs. Peacock from the Billiard Room to the Lounge, the answer to the mystery of whodunit, where and how, if not why, just a roll of the die away.

Sto Lat. The eighth stanza's italicized segment is taken from Robert Desnos' eponymous poem, "The Voice of Robert Desnos" (trans., Carolyn Forché and William Kulik). The Gestapo arrested Desnos in 1944 because of his activities in support of the French Resistance. He died of typhus at Terezin in 1945, as World War II was ending.

Passover. Upon the dissolution of the Ottoman Empire in the early part of the 20th century, cosmopolitan and polyglot Smyrna became Izmir, Turkey. *"Ochi Tchornya,"* or "Dark Eyes," is a well-known Russian folk song about the yearning for, and impossibility of, love across cultures.

ABOUT THE AUTHOR

Roy Jacobstein is a pediatrician and public health physician working in the field of international health. He was educated at the University of Michigan and University of Rochester. After residing in Washington, DC, where he was an official of the U.S. Agency for International Development, he now lives in Chapel Hill, NC. His poems have appeared in many literary magazines, periodicals and newspapers including *Witness*, the *Washington Post*, the *Threepenny Review*, *Quarterly West*, *Puerto del Sol*, *Prarie Schooner*, and *Poetry Northwest*. He is the recipient of *Mid-American Review's* 1999 James Wright Poetry Prize, and is completing his MFA at Warren Wilson College.

North Carolina Writers' Network Chapbook Series:

1985—*Carolina Shout!* by Shelby Stephenson
    (Playwrights' Fund of North Carolina)

1986—*Satan Speaks of Eve in Seven Voices, After the Fall*
    by Anna Wooten-Hawkins

1987—*Oriflamb* by Isabel Zuber

1988—*A Rapid Transit* by Edison Dupree

1989—*Off-Road Meditations* by Becky Gould Gibson

1990—*What the Welsh and Chinese Have in Common* by Paul Jones

1991—*Memories of Light* by Robin Greene

1992—*Staying In* by Grey Brown

1993—*New River* by Gail Peck

1994—*The Everlasting Universe of Things* by Kathleen Halme

1995—*The Tan Chantuese* by Carol Boston Weatherford

1996—*Tea Leaves* by Louise Cary Barden

1997—*Back to Back* by Debra Kang Dean

1998—*Figments of the Firmament* by Margaret Rabb

1999—*City of the Moon* by Maria Hummel